Wise El
on

SURVIVING RECESSIONS
DEPRESSIONS & DOWNTURNS

30 Effective Tips To Help You Get Through Some Of Life's Lessons

by

Euphrosene Labon

Surviving Recessions Depressions & Downturns

Surviving Recessions Depressions & Downturns

By the same author:

A Little Book of Big Sales Tips
A Little Book of Self-Publishing Tips
A Little Book of Self-Coaching Tips
A Little Book of Time Tips
A Little Book of Abundance Tips
Profit From Unlimited Thinking

This book is available to order
as a print book from all good bookshops
as well as Amazon.
It may also be purchased directly
from the publisher.

Additionally, it is available
at quantity discounts for bulk purchase
for business, educational
or sales promotional use.

Please email
euphrosene@euphrosenelabon.com
for more information.

Surviving Recessions Depressions & Downturns

WISE EL
ON
SURVIVING RECESSIONS DEPRESSIONS & DOWNTURNS

BY

EUPHROSENE LABON

FLOREO PUBLISHING
ANGMERING WEST SUSSEX

Surviving Recessions Depressions & Downturns

First published in Great Britain in 2005 by
Floreo Publishing
Brambletye close
Angmering
West Sussex
BN16 4DD

ISBN-13 978-1-905402-07-6

General/NON-Fiction/ How-to

A catalogue record for this book
is available from the British Library
Design and word processing
Floreo Publishing

Additional distribution:
http://www.euphroseneLabon.com
Email: euphrosene@euphrosenelabon.com

Surviving Recessions Depressions & Downturns

INTRODUCTION

Wise El is the latest incarnation in my quest to inform and teach in the easiest possible way.

Still retaining the one-liner philosophy of the previous Little Books, now there are cartoons to make it easier still to take in information.

Wise El is the main character, whose journey, questioning, experiencing and learning, is shared by a variety of other cartoon sentients.

In this book, Wise El has picked the main tips needed to survive most kinds of financial downturn.

I hope any downturn you may be facing is brief and that you can spot the light that is or will be there eventually.

Have courage!

Euphrosene Labon
Angmering 2011

Surviving Recessions Depressions & Downturns

Listen and learn from someone who has experienced the same before.

Surviving Recessions Depressions & Downturns

Don't be too proud. Do any job that might help you on to the right path.

Surviving Recessions Depressions & Downturns

Learn how to barter,
haggle
and bargain.

Surviving Recessions Depressions & Downturns

Diversify.
Don't put
all your eggs
in one basket.

Surviving Recessions Depressions & Downturns

Love yourself.
Discover your inner wealth.
Improve your skills.

Surviving Recessions Depressions & Downturns

Keep busy!

Surviving Recessions Depressions & Downturns

Everything passes.

Surviving Recessions Depressions & Downturns

Try to save a little regularly.
create an emergency fund.

Surviving Recessions Depressions & Downturns

Make do
and mend.
Patch, sew and
fix it.

Surviving Recessions Depressions & Downturns

cut down on all unnecessary expenditure.

Surviving Recessions Depressions & Downturns

Free your mind.
Escape
in your imagination.

Surviving Recessions Depressions & Downturns

Don't bottle up your feelings. Talk to someone.

Surviving Recessions Depressions & Downturns

Always
look
on the bright
side.
It will
improve
your
wellbeing.

Surviving Recessions Depressions & Downturns

Do
as you would be
done by.
Help someone else.

Surviving Recessions Depressions & Downturns

Be useful.
Provide a service
that helps others
or lightens
their load.

Surviving Recessions Depressions & Downturns

Be creative
with your cooking.
Become a genius
with leftovers.

Surviving Recessions
Depressions & Downturns

cut up
your credit cards
unless you are
very disciplined.

Surviving Recessions Depressions & Downturns

change
your values.
Develop
positive
character
traits.
Reach
for the stars.

Surviving Recessions Depressions & Downturns

count your blessings.
crises happen
to all of us.
It's how you handle them
that matters.

Surviving Recessions Depressions & Downturns

Be innovative.
Find a need
and fill it.
Create something
that other people need.

Surviving Recessions Depressions & Downturns

Talk
to your suppliers.
Negotiate
a payment plan.
Always communicate.

Surviving Recessions Depressions & Downturns

Speculate - but only if you can afford to lose the money.

Surviving Recessions Depressions & Downturns

Don't keep your head down.
Blow your own trumpet.
Get out there and network.

Surviving Recessions Depressions & Downturns

Don't borrow money
if you are already up to your
neck in debt - unless you are
consolidating what you
already owe.
Take advice first though.

PROMISED LAND

DEBT MOUNTAIN

Surviving Recessions
Depressions & Downturns

Do sell off
all unnecessary
possessions.

Surviving Recessions
Depressions & Downturns

Learn something new.
It will open up your mind
to other opportunities.

Surviving Recessions
Depressions & Downturns

Develop a sense of
humour.
You cannot laugh
and feel fear
at the same time.

Surviving Recessions Depressions & Downturns

Don't buy anything you cannot afford.

Surviving Recessions Depressions & Downturns

Never give up.
Never give up.
Never give up.

Surviving Recessions Depressions & Downturns

Live simply.
Take time
to smell the roses.

Surviving Recessions Depressions & Downturns

USEFUL READING

Discover Yourself – Lillian Too
Prosperity – Charles Fillmore
Think Yourself Rich – Joseph Murphy
Open Your Mind To Prosperity – Catherine Ponder
Rich Dad, Poor Dad – Robert Kiyosaki
Money Wisdom – Carolyn Temsi & Caro Handey
The Seven Laws of Money – Michael Phillips
Creating Money – Roman/Packer
The Wisdom of James Allen
Creative Abundance – Elizabeth Clare Prophet
The Abundance Book – John Randolph Price
In Tune With The Infinite – Ralph Waldo Trine
The Lazy Man's Way To Riches – Joe Karbo
The Master Key – Charles F Haanel
Find And Use Your Inner Power – Emmet Fox
How to Get Out of Debt, Stay Out of Debt, and Live
Prosperously: *(Based on the Proven Principles and
Techniques of Debtors Anonymous) – Jerrold Mundis
10 Minute Guide to Beating Debt – Susan Abentrod

Surviving Recessions Depressions & Downturns

QUOTATIONS TO HELP YOU SURVIVE

The only real security that a man will have in this world in a reserve of knowledge, experience and ability. - **Henry Ford**

Faith is the evidence of things not seen… - **St Paul**

Mind is the creator of everything. If you cling to a certain thought with dynamic will power, it finally assumes a tangible outward form. – **Paramahansa Yogananda**

Henceforth I ask not good fortune. I myself am good fortune. - **Walt Whitman**

By learning the laws of mind, you can extract from that infinite storehouse within you everything you need in order to live life gloriously, joyously and abundantly. - **Joseph Murphy**

You can have prosperity no matter what your present circumstances may be. The Law gives you power to attain prosperity and position without infringing the rights and opportunities of anyone else in the world. - **Emmet Fox**

It is the fear of this or that, that prevents a channel from making for the greater supply. - **Edgar Cayce**

Surviving Recessions Depressions & Downturns

He who refreshes others will himself be refreshed. - **Proverbs 11.25**

When you believe in what you create you will find people who are willing to pay for your creations. **– Carolyn Temsi & Caro Handley**

The true prosperity is not the accumulation of great wealth. To be truly prosperous is to have the use of enough to enable one to live without struggling and yet to be free from the joyless burden of wealth. **– Henry Thomas Hamblin**

In your mind see plenty everywhere. Yes, it is hard sometimes to overcome the thought that there is not enough, for it is an insidious thought that has been in consciousness for a long time. **– Charles Fillmore**

Through humor, you can soften some of the worst blows that life delivers. And once you find laughter, no matter how painful your situation might be, you can survive it. **– Bill Cosby**

Man can live about forty days without food, about three days without water, about eight minutes without air, but only for one second without hope **- Anon**

Surviving Recessions Depressions & Downturns

It is not the strongest of the species that survives, nor the most intelligent that survives. It is the one that is the most adaptable to change. **– Charles Darwin**

Live within your means, never be in debt, and by husbanding your money you can always lay it out well. But when you get in debt you become a slave. Therefore I say to you never involve yourself in debt, and become no man's surety. If your friend is in distress, aid him if you have the means to spare. If he fails to be able to return it, it is only so much lost. - **Andrew Jackson**

Rather go to bed supperless than rise in debt. - **Benjamin Franklin**

As sure as the spring will follow the winter, prosperity and economic growth will follow recession. - **Bo Bennett**

Surviving Recessions Depressions & Downturns

BRIEF BIOG

Euphrosene Labon is an artist, writer and author whose enthusiasm for learning and sharing her experience has also made her create a small publishing house. Make that a very small publishing house.

Her earlier career was predominantly in IT, as a successful sales and business development executive. Prior to that, she spent many years in training.

Euphrosene's main aim with her writings is to share the knowledge she has gained – and, hopefully, to make it easier for others to pursue and achieve their goals.

As well as the Little Book series, she has written Profit From Unlimited Thinking – a unique blend of timeless spiritual wisdom and business sense to help the reader transcend any limitations, in easy-to-follow steps.

She shares her spiritual journey, warts and all, through Delusions of Divinity?, her blog. To read more, please visit
http://www.euphroselabon.com/modules/wordpress/

Surviving Recessions Depressions & Downturns

This book is available in print form, at quantity discounts, for bulk purchase for business, educational or sales promotional use.

To discuss your requirements or for further information please email euphrosene@euphrosenelabon.com or call 07803 724963.

www.ingramcontent.com/pod-product-compliance
Lightning Source LLC
Chambersburg PA
CBHW060633030426
42337CB00018B/3344